The Holy Land from Past to Present—a Primer for Tayarim, Talmidim, Vatikim, Noodnikim, and Dreamers

For the *Love* of Israel

Written by RABBI STEVEN STARK LOWENSTEIN   Illustrated and designed by MARK ANDERSON

One does

ONE ASCENDS THE ROAD TAKEN BY GENERATIONS...ONE BRINGS RUCKSACKS

not travel

STUFFED WITH MEMORIES TO EACH MOUNTAIN AND EACH HILL...ONE OFFERS

to Jerusalem.

A BLESSING FOR MEMORIES OF THE PAST WHICH HAVE BEEN RENEWED.

One returns.

~ Yitzhak Yasinowitz

THE METEORIC RISE OF THE STATE OF ISRAEL IN 1948 FROM THE ASHES OF EUROPE IS BEYOND INSPIRING.

Its continued survival against all odds and its very existence is a direct result of the unequalled dedication and determination of some seven million residents, each one caring deeply for this tiny plot of land after just six decades of Statehood. Israelis love their culture and are passionate about their political system. Their survival is never taken for granted.

Israel is a land of unbelievable contrasts and short distances, a country whose tumultuous existence often overshadows the rich and vibrant life within it. Israel is a land of incredible beauty, character, and variety. It is where the world's religions were born and passionate battles were fought to protect them.

For many, Israel has become synonymous with conflict and terror. Yet beneath the surface, this tiny stretch of land inspires an incredible mesh of beliefs, weaving a tapestry of beauty unlike anywhere else in the world. Thanks to its millions of immigrants, many different faiths, and numerous cultures, Israel's uniqueness shines forth. Whether you have been to Israel once or many times, we hope you enjoy this journey from past to present and from present to past.

"A" is for *Aliyah,*

To go up a steep ascent
Following in the footsteps of *Abraham,*
Who crossed over the Fertile Crescent.

According to tradition, traveling to the Land of Israel is an ascent, both geographically and metaphysically. Anyone traveling to Eretz Israel from Egypt, Babylonia, or the Mediterranean basin (where many Jews lived in early rabbinic times), climbed to a higher altitude. In 1933, David Wolfsohn was given the task of creating a flag for the Jewish State to be unveiled at the Zionist congress. He chose a combination of the Magen David (the star/shield of David) and the tallit (the traditional prayer shawl). The sky-blue color is said to evoke the presence of God. The interlocking triangles point in all directions, forever linking the past and the future. The beauty of Israel…always look up.

"Once I sat on the steps by a gate at David's Tower, I placed my two heavy baskets at my side. A group of tourists was standing around their guide and I became their target marker. 'You see that man with the baskets? Just right of his head there's an arch from the Roman period. Just right of his head.' 'But he's moving, he's moving!' I said to myself: redemption will come only if their guide tells them, 'You see that arch from the Roman period? It's not important: but next to it, left and down a bit, there sits a man who's bought fruit and vegetables for his family.'" ~**Tourists** *by Yehuda Amechai*

"B" is for

"In Israel, in order to be a realist you must believe in miracles."

"This country made us a people; our people made this a country."

~*David Ben-Gurion*

Birth*right*,

A privilege, a heritage, a right
To eat *Bissli* and *Bamba*
With never a fear or fright.

Bamba has been Israel's most popular snack food since it was first created in 1963. It controls 25 percent of the snack-food market in Israel. Made with peanut butter–flavored stuffed corn, it has been called cheese doodles without the cheese. Its rival Bissli comes in many different flavors and many different shapes. Biss means "bite," li means "for me."

"The source of our friendship runs deeper than any treaty. It is grounded in the shared spirit of our people. The bonds of the book, the ties of the soul." ~*George W. Bush*

"C" is for the Chalutzim,

The pioneers who changed our way.
Like "Our Man in Damascus"
and *Omri Casspi* in the NBA.

The early Chalutzim who came to Israel to drain swamps and make the desert bloom considered themselves revolutionaries. They had not come just to change the condition of the land, but also to change themselves. They were aiming for a revolution in the character of the entire Jewish people. They came to the country to transform it, and in so doing, they transformed themselves. *Eli Cohen* was a Jewish Egyptian recruited in 1960 by the Mossad (Israel's secret service) to become a special agent in Damascus. Living under the name Kamel Amin Tsa'abet, he infiltrated the highest levels of Syrian intelligence and sent crucial messages back to the Mossad to aid the Israeli effort. In 1965 his radio message was intercepted, and he was caught and publically hanged in Damascus.

Omri Casspi, in 2009, became the first Israeli selected in the first round of the National Basketball Association draft. The Sacramento Kings selected him with the the 23rd pick in the draft. In the Jewish world, a 6-foot, 9-inch small forward is a GIANT and is looked up to by 99.9 percent of population. And he can jump!

"America and Israel share a special bond. Our relationship is unique among all nations. Like America, Israel is a strong democracy, a symbol of freedom, and an oasis of liberty, a home to the oppressed and persecuted." ~ *Bill Clinton*

"D" is for Degania,

The country's first collective farm.
On this kibbutz *Moshe Dayan* was born;
A hero filled with bravery and charm.

Moshe Dayan belonged to a new generation of tough, home-grown military commanders. He was born in 1915 to Shmuel Dayan, a member of Degania, the very first kibbutz, which was located near the Sea of Galilee. He joined the Haganah in his teens and in 1941 lost an eye in an operation against French forces in Lebanon. Beginning in 1948, Dayan held many positions in the Israel Defense Forces. He was chief of staff and a minister of defense during the 1967 War. Besides his military career, Dayan was a farmer, a secret poet, an amateur archaeologist, a politician, and a statesman who usually spoke briefly and to the point—a rarity for any politician, especially an Israeli one.

"Israel and the Palestinians must resolve their own differences. The United States can play an important role as facilitator and guarantor." ~*Alan Dershowitz*

Ein bayah Not a problem   Eretz Yisrael The Land of Israel   Erev tov Good evening   Efshar Possible   Etgar Challenge

Eifo hasherutim? Where is the bathroom?   Esser A perfect 10

"E" is for Elite,

Scrumptious and delicious candy.
The chocolate is always tasty
And coffee always quite dandy.

Eliyahu Fromenchenko started making chocolate in his home kitchen in Latvia in 1918. He made his way to Israel in 1933, bought land in Ramat Gan near Tel Aviv, and began making chocolate—lots and lots of chocolate. In 1958 Elite branched out into coffee. Coffee in Israel is serious business. Israelis don't just drink coffee, they appreciate it. In Israel you don't "grab a cup of coffee." Instead, you sit down, take it slow, and *enjoy* a cup of coffee. In the army, coffee is made in a finjan right in the open fire. In Israel, you can enjoy Turkish coffee, botz or "mud coffee," and Nescafé. (In Hebrew *nes* means "miracle," so in Israel instant coffee was thought to be a miracle.) No matter where you look, you will not find a Starbucks: Starbucks coffee just doesn't have enough caffeine to jolt this society.

"One can be an internationalist without being indifferent to the members of one's tribe. The Zionist cause is very close to my heart. . . . I am glad that there should be a little patch of earth on which our kindred brethren are not considered aliens."

~*Albert Einstein*

"F" is for Falafel,

The country's most famous fast food.
But don't be surprised when the waiter who serves it
Is opinionated, obnoxious, or rude.

Yummy...Israel is a smorgasbord of different traditions, styles, religions, and nationalities...all cooking together in the same kitchen using very different recipes. Yet the common ingredient is the chickpea, used for hummus and falafel. Hummus is a thick and rich puree of chickpeas, tahini oil, lemon juice, and garlic served with fresh, piping-hot pita bread. Falafel is ground-up, spicy chickpea balls (ping-pong size) deep fried and served with hummus and salads. This is Israeli fast food. Throw in shakshouka (eggs, tomatoes, onions, and peppers) for breakfast, shawarma (slow-roasted, spiced lamb) for lunch, and bourekas (pastry puffs stuffed with cheese, meat, veggies, or potatoes) for dinner. And don't forget some chocolate rugelach for dessert. By the way, eating a falafel without dripping the various ingredients on your chin, shirt, or shoes can only be mastered by natives!

"The Israelis have more courage in their pinky finger that I have in my whole life. Going to the supermarket in Eretz Yisroel is an act of courage." ~ *Tovah Feldshuh*

"G" is for *Galilee*

and Golan Heights,

A mountainous region quite rocky;
And for teacher and politician *Golda Meir*
The greatest import from Milwaukee.

The lush and fertile Galilee and the mountainous Golan Heights are two of the most beautiful and most traveled parts of Israel. Both regions are filled with scenic treasures as well as lovely nature reserves, historic sites, and archaeological wonders. The natural beauty and breathtaking landscapes make these areas unique and wondrous.

"God said to Abraham: 'Go forth from your native land and from your father's house to the land that I will show you. I will make of you a great nation, and I will bless you; I will make your name great, and you shall be a blessing.'"

~*Genesis 12:1*

"I am a Jew and like my ancestors, I long for Zion and Jerusalem. It doesn't have to be perfect. It just has to be. It is prayer that keeps the dream alive." ~*Ari L. Goldman*

"H" is for
Hebrew,

One of the oldest languages still spoken,
And for Zionist thinker *Theodor Herzl,*
Whose dream has never been broken.

Israel is one of the world's youngest countries speaking perhaps the oldest language. Spoken Hebrew was dead for a couple thousand years. It was kept alive only through study of the Torah and prayer. When the great Zionist dream began in the 19ᵗ century, Hebrew again was taught and spoken. Thus the vision of *Eleazar Ben Yehuda,* originator of the modern idea of the nation of Israel reborn in its own land and with its own language, has come true.

"When I go to Israel every stone and every tree is a reminder of hard labor and glory, of prophets and psalmists, of loyalty and holiness. The Jews go to Israel not only for physical security for themselves, and their children; they go to Israel for renewal, for the experience of resurrection…. Israel enables us to bear the agony of Auschwitz without radical despair, to sense a ray of God's radiance in the jungles of history." *~Abraham Joshua Heschel*

"At Basel, I founded the Jewish State. If I said this out loud today, I would be answered by universal laughter. If not in five years, certainly in 50, everyone will know it." ~ *Theodor Herzl, diaries, 1897*

"I" is for # Ilan,

The astronaut who flew through space.

But if you really want to see a miracle,

Independence Hall is the place.

The home of *Zina* and *Meir Dizengoff* was one of the first houses built in Tel Aviv. It was chosen to host the Declaration of the State on Friday May 14, 1948. Those who received an invitation didn't even know what they were attending. A few minutes after 4 PM, David Ben-Gurion read Israel's Declaration of Independence, the band played *Hatikvah*, and the rabbi said a prayer. With seven hostile armies poised to attack the very next day, the joy and celebration of Statehood was short-lived. The Dizengoff home is now known as Independence Hall.

"The State if Israel will be open for Jewish immigration and for the Ingathering of the Exiles; it will foster the development of the country for the benefit of all its inhabitants; it will be based on freedom, justice, and peace as envisaged by the prophets of Israel; it will ensure complete equality of social and political rights to all its inhabitants irrespective of religion, race, or sex; it will guarantee freedom of religion, conscience, language, education, and culture; it will safeguard the Holy Places of all religions." *~Israel's Declaration of Independence*

In 1997, Colonel *Ilan Ramon* was selected by NASA to serve as a payload specialist on the Space Shuttle *Columbia*; he was the first Israeli astronaut. The seven-member crew launched on January 16, 2003, for a 16-day mision. During the mission, Ramon conducted a number of experiments, and the flight was considered a great success. He said, *"Being the first Israeli astronaut—I feel I am representing all Jews and all Israelis.… I'm the son of a Holocaust survivor—I carry on the suffering of the Holocaust generation, and I'm proof that despite all the horror they went through, we're going forward."* Kosher meals were provided by NASA for his journey and he consulted with rabbis before leaving about the proper way to observe Shabbat in space. Ramon carried poems, photographs, and letters as well as a credit card–size microfiche copy of the Torah. He also took a pencil drawing titled "Moon Landscape" by a 14-year-old Jewish boy, Peter Ginz, killed at Auschwitz. Ramon was a national hero and a symbol of hope. Tragically, minutes before landing, *Columbia* exploded, killing everyone on board. May Ilan Ramon's memory be for a blessing and inspire us all to reach for the sky.

J

Jerusalem is a city of contrasts: Jews, Muslims, Christians; ancient and new neighborhoods; houses of prayer of all communities and religions; tourists filling the streets and alleys. First and foremost, from the viewpoint of most Israelis and Jews, it is the present and eternal capital of Israel. *Naomi Shemer*, the first lady of song in Israel, composed many beautiful lyrics and poems. Her most famous was "Jerusalem of Gold," released just before the start of the Six-Day War in 1967. "Jerusalem of gold, and of bronze and of light, I am an instrument for all your songs..."

Jerus

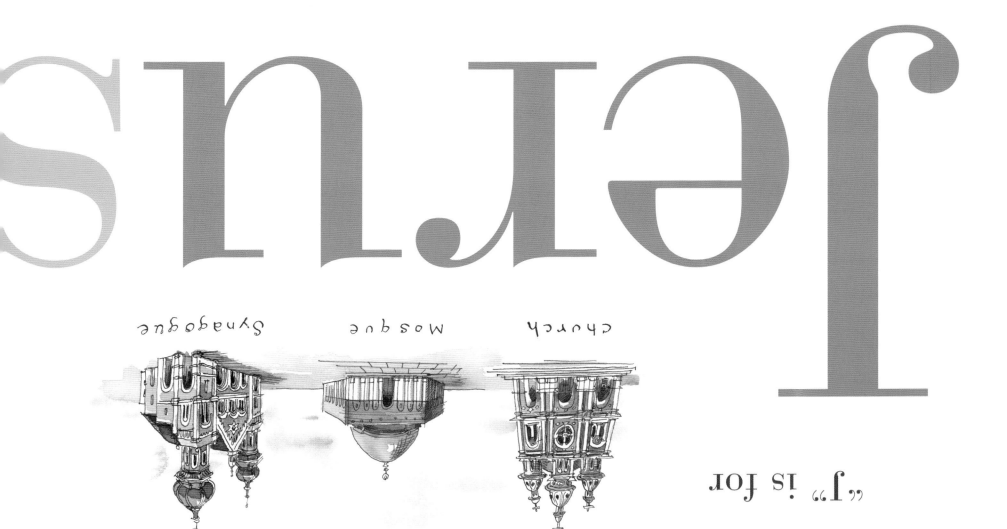

Church   Mosque   Synagogue

"It was Friday—"Erev Shabbat"—when we arrived.
The Sabbath Queen was quickly approaching and the entire city was preparing for the arrival of the
royal guest. Everywhere, stores were closing and public transportation was coming to a halt.
As the siren was sounded, stillness descended on the Holy City. Suddenly, scores of people spilled into the streets.
They came from every direction: young and old, men and women, Israelis and tourists, students and soldiers, pious Hasidim in
long black coats, and Westernized Jews in business suits. They came from the four corners of the world; they spoke in many tongues
and espoused many ideas. Wondrously, they all merged into one—all rushing, running to the same place,
to the Western Wall. I came close to the wall and poured out my soul.
A gentle breeze was in the air and a wonderful serenity descended upon me.
I looked up at the foliage sprouting from the crevices.
Strange how these little flowers grow without being watered by the tears of a nation
that had been waiting for two thousand years."

~Rebbetzin Esther Jungreis

alem

ירושלים

"K" is for the

Knes*set*,

Politics from the center, left, and right.
Parties are formed by anyone
And change from morning to night.

It is said that during Golda Meir's term as prime minister, she made her most important decisions sitting in her kitchen with just a few advisors—thus the term "kitchen cabinet," a place many important politicians want to be. Israel is a parliamentary democracy with legislative, executive, and judicial branches. The head of the state is the president, whose duties are mostly ceremonial and formal; the office symbolizes the unity and sovereignty of the State. The Knesset, Israel's legislative authority, is a 120-member unicameral parliament, which "hopefully" operates in plenary session. In Israel, it doesn't take much to start a political party; at any given time there could be 40 different parties vying for seats.

"Israel is the child of hope and the home of the brave." *~John F. Kennedy*

" Israel is one of the great outposts of democracy in the world, and a marvelous example of what can be done, how desert land can be transformed into an oasis of brotherhood and democracy. Peace for Israel means security and that security must be a reality." *~Rev. Martin Luther King, Jr.*

Lehitraot See ya soon   Lama Why   Lo No   Lama lo Why not   Lila tov Good night   Lo ba li I don't feel like it   Lifamim Sometimes

Libriut To your health   La-gam-rai Totally

"L" is for the *Land*

That flows with milk and honey
And music...and art...
And comedians who are quite funny.

Israel loves music. The Israeli Philharmonic Orchestra gave its very first concert in Tel Aviv under the baton of *Arturo Toscanini* in December 1936 and for many years has been inspired by musical director *Zubin Mehta*. Sometimes it is a simple accordian player leading barefoot Israeli dancers that expresses boundless joy. Or it could be Chasidic singer *Matisyahu*, the *Idan Raichel Project* blending Ethiopian and western music, psychedelic trance group *Infected Mushroom*, or greats like *Naomi Shemer* and *David Broza* lifting Israel's culture and music to high notes. *Kochav Hanolad*—"A Star is Born" (since "Israel Idol" would violate several basic commandments)— had its first Ethiopian winner, *Hagit Yasou*.

Ephraim Kishon's column in the Israeli daily *Maariv* was largely political and social satire. His books have been translated into 37 different languages. He once wrote: "Israel is the only country in the world where 'small talk' consists of loud, angry debate over politics and religion. Israel is the only country in the world where one is unlikely to dig a cellar without hitting ancient archaeological artifacts. Israel is the only country in the world where the leading writers in the country take buses. Israel is the only country in the world where the graffiti is in Hebrew. Israel is the only country in the world where patients visiting physicians end up giving the doctor advice. Israel is the only country in the world where everyone strikes up conversations while waiting in lines."

"We do not rejoice in victories. We rejoice when a new kind of cotton is grown and when strawberries bloom in Israel." ~ *Golda Meir*

Mitzuyan Excellent   Metek Cutie   Mishpacha Family   Meshuga Crazy person   Mayim Water   Misadah Restaurant

Memshallah Government   Moreh derech Tour guide   Ma nishma? Whats up?   Magniv Awesome   Maspeek Enough

"M" is for

Megiddo

and

Masada,

Unique places you surely can't miss.
But in your local corner *Makolet*
You'll find your food-shopping bliss.

Megiddo is an ancient biblical mound containing more than 30 levels of civilization on an important ancient and modern crossroad. By the third millennium BCE, Megiddo was a powerfully fortified city; 1,000 years later it became a center of Egyptian rule and is mentioned frequently in the Bible. No doubt there is a connection between Armageddon, the end of the world, and Har Megidoo. The fortress of Masada overlooking the Dead Sea was King Herod's vacation property, though Herod never took a vacation. Masada was where 973 zealots chose to inhabit after the siege of Jerusalem in the year 70 CE. For three years they held off the Roman Legion, choosing to die as free people rather than fall into the hands of the Romans. Masada is a symbol of strength and perseverance for Israeli soldiers…and for tourists who try to hike up the winding Snake Path approach to the fortress in 40 minutes or less.

"N" is for the

Netanyahu *brothers,*

Bibi and Yoni, no doubt.

Yoni was the hero of Entebbe,
Bibi the politician with clout.

Operation Thunderbolt: *Yonatan Netanyahu* was the commander of an elite unit of Israeli commandos who traveled 2,500 miles in 1976 to storm the airport in Entebbe, Uganda, to free Israelis on a hijacked Air France jet. Yoni was the only soldier killed in the operation.

"As I don't intend to tell my grandchildren about the Jewish State in the 20th century as a mere brief and transient episode in thousands of years of wandering, I intend to hold on here with all my might." ~*Yonatan Netanyahu*

"My first name, Benjamin, dates back a thousand years earlier to Binyamin, the son of Jacob, who was also known as Israel. Jacob and his 12 sons roamed these same hills 4,000 years ago, and there's been a continuous Jewish presence in the land ever since." ~*Benjamin Netanyahu*

"O" is for the many

Operations

Bringing immigrants here safe and sound.

From Morocco and Yemen and Ethiopia,

They cried when their planes touched the ground.

Operation Magic Carpet brought 49,000 Yemenite Jews to Israel in 1949–1950.
Operation Opera prevented Iraq from developing nuclear weapons and weapons of mass destruction by bombing the country's nuclear reactor in 1981. Operation Moses evacuated more than 8,000 Beta Yisrael during the 1984 Sudan famine. Operation Solomon transported 14,325 Ethiopian Jews over a 36-hour period in 1991.

"Our bond with Israel is unbreakable. It is the bond of two peoples that share a commitment to a common set of ideals: opportunity, democracy, and freedom."

~Barack Obama

P is for

שלום

"Pray for the peace of Jerusalem:
May those who love you be secure.
May there be peace within your walls
and security within your citadels.
For the sake of my family and friends,
I will say, 'Peace be within you.'"
~*Psalm 122*

"Israel is . . . Where I was born.

Where I ate my first Popsicle and used a proper toilet for the first time.

Where some of my 18-year-old friends spend their nights in bunkers sleeping with their helmets on.

Where security guards are the only jobs in surplus.

Where deserts bloom and pioneer stories are sentimentalized.

Where a thorny, sweet cactus is the symbol of the ideal Israeli.

Where immigrating to Israel is called 'ascending' and emigrating from Israel is called 'descending.'

Where my grandparents were not born, but where they were saved.

Where the muezzin chants, and the church bells sound, and the shofars cry freely at the Wall.

Where the shopkeepers bargain. Where the politicians bargain.

Where there will one day be peace, but never quiet.

Where I was born; where my insides refuse to abandon."

~Natalie Portman

Q is for *The Caves of*

Qumran,

An area of deserts and hills
Where a young boy found his treasure
And archaeologists honed their skills.

In the spring of 1947, a Bedouin boy searching the cliffs along the Dead Sea for a lost goat came upon a cave containing large jars filled with manuscripts. They were sold for a small amount to a cobbler and antiquities dealer named Kando, who later sold three of the scrolls to *Eleazar L. Sukenik* of Hebrew University. This find caused a sensation when it was revealed to the world and it continues to fascinate scholars and the public to this day. Between 1949 and 1956, thousands of fragments of scrolls and remnants of roughly 800 manuscripts dating from approximately 200 BCE to 68 CE were found. Included in this discovery were some of the oldest known surviving copies of biblical and extra-biblical documents preserving evidence of the great diversity in late Second Temple Judaism. The Dead Sea Scrolls are written in Hebrew, Aramaic, and Greek, mostly on parchment, and are now housed at The Shrine of the Book in Jerusalem's Israel Museum.

"R" is for the

Roths*childs*,

Whose deep pockets built the State,
And for *Rachel* the poetess,
A Zionist dreamer first rate.

Baron Edmond de Rothschild, the philanthropist, was a wealthy French Jew whose family roots were traced to Germany. Luckily, he wasn't interested in the family banking business and began helping Jews flee from the pogroms of eastern Europe. He established a haven for them in the Holy Land starting in 1882. He was instrumental in the building of more than 30 moshavot, villages, and settlements in the Land of Israel, funding them almost entirely from his own money and naming them after himself or members of his family. Among the first settlements were Rishon LeZion, Zichron Yaakov, Gedera, Rosh Pina, and Mazkeret Batya. He became the honorary president of the Jewish Agency in 1929.

Rachel Bluwstein (1890–1931), a poet known simply as Rachel, was born in Russia and came to Palestine in 1909 as a pioneer. She left to study agriculture in 1913, but when she returned with tuberculosis, after World War I, she was unable to resume the difficult pioneer life in the Galilee. Her lyric poetry reflects the melancholy sensitivity of a doomed young woman, yearning for the life she was unable to lead.

"And perhaps these things never were, and perhaps, I never rose at dawn to the garden to work it by the sweat of my brow. Never, not on long and blazing days of harvest on top of a cart full of sheaf. I did not raise my voice in song. I never washed in the peaceful azure and innocence of my Kinneret…oh my Kinneret did you exist, or did I dream a dream." ~*Rachel*

"To give you an idea how small that is, you could take more than 30 Israels and put them together and the whole thing would still be smaller than Texas. There may be counties, even ranches, in Texas that are bigger.... We're really talking dinky. Why during any really cold winter you can find more Jews in South Florida." ~*Mike Royko*

"I'm always in favor of Israel responding strongly when it's threatened. At the same time, a response to a response doesn't really solve anything. It just creates a perpetual-motion machine." ~*Steven Spielberg*

"S" is for

Hannah Szenes,

Whose short life was an inspiration.
It's also for a short list of Israeli athletes
Who bask in their own perspiration.

Israel has enjoyed some sports success, with Macabee Tel Aviv winning the European basketball cup several times (thanks, Tal Brody) and the national soccer team qualifying for the World Cup in 1970. Matkot, Israel's unofficial national sport, gets played every day on the beaches of Tel Aviv and beyond; in the game, a rubber ball gets smashed by two wooden racquets. Matkot requires quick reflexes and seems best played in a very tight, low-cut Speedo. Israeli medals in the Olympics have been few, limited to just sailing, judo, and canoeing. Sadly, 11 members of Israel's 1972 team were killed in Munich in the worst terrorist attack in Olympic history. *David Berger, Ze'ev Friedman, Yossef Romano, Eliezer Halfin, Yossef Gutfreund, Amitzur Shapira, Kehat Shorr, Mark Slavin, Andre Spitzer, Yakov Springer*, and *Moshe Weinberg* are sports heroes who will never be forgotten.

"Oh God, my God, I pray that these things never end. The sand and the sea, the rush of the water, the crash of the heavens, the prayer of the heart." *~Hannah Szenes*, Walk to Caesarea, 1943

"T" is for

Technology,

Key to this "startup" nation:
A country founded on chutzpah,
Perspiration, imagination, and exploration.

Israelis, for the most part, don't believe in miracles, yet they rely on them on a regular basis. Today, Israel's high-tech economy is booming. Israel is a country of immigrants, and immigrants are known to be great entrepreneurs. Israel is the second-best region in the world for venture-backed companies after Silicon Valley. It ranks third among countries, after the United States and China, with the most companies on the U.S. stock exchanges. Despite being a highly urbanized western country, poverty levels remain pretty high. Israel is known for a very high cost of living, but the good news is that the bank allows you to withdraw double your salary each month. Israel has more than just "haves" and "have nots." The country actually has a new group: "have not paid for what they have."

"One of the proudest days of my life occurred at 6:12 PM on Friday, May 14, 1948, when I was able to announce recognition of the new State of Israel by the government of the United States. In view of the long friendship of the American people for the Zionist ideal, it was particularly appropriate that our government should be the first to recognize the new state."

~ *Harry S. Truman*

"The world's beauty is divided into ten equal parts. Nine parts came to Jerusalem and one part to the rest of the world."

~*The Talmud*

"U" is for Ukraine,

Where *Yitzchak Rabin's* father was born.
Rabin's sudden and shocking assassination
Caused the whole wide world to mourn.

Yitzchak Rabin—politician, statesman, and general—was the fifth prime minister of Israel and the first native-born prime minister. He served two terms in office, 1974–77 and 1992 until his assassination in 1995. In 1994, he—along with Shimon Peres and Yasser Arafat—won the Nobel Peace Prize after the signing of the Oslo Peace Accords. During the 1967 War he was one of the first to enter the Old City and recaptured the Temple Mount. It was at Rabin's funeral that President Bill Clinton poignantly said, "Shalom, chaver". . . good-bye and peace, my friend.

"We must think differently, look at things in a different way. Peace requires a world of new concepts, new definitions."
"You don't make peace with friends. You make it with very unsavory enemies." ~ *Yitzchak Rabin*

"V" is for the **Via Dolorosa**,

From *Gethsemane to Golgatha*
Where Jesus walked through the stages.
History gets told and retold through the ages.

The Via Dolorosa, Latin for "way of grief," is the street within the Old City of Jerusalem held to be the path that Jesus walked, carrying his cross, on the way to his crucifixion. For as long as Christians have been coming to this holy city, they have walked the 14 stations of the cross, beginning at the Antonia Fortress and concluding at the Church of the Holy Sepulchre. Since the Middle Ages, the Franciscans, who have greatly contributed to the elaboration of pilgrimage traditions, walk the Via Dolorosa every Friday afternoon, bearing a heavy wooden cross.

Vaik Veteran   Vered Rose   Va'ad Committee

"W" is for Water,
A national obsession,
And for the *Western Wall*,
A place for spiritual expression.

The scarcity of water in Israel has generated intense efforts to maximize the use of available supply and to seek new resources. In the 1960s, Israel's freshwater sources were joined in an integrated grid whose main artery, the National Water Carrier, brings water from the north and center of the country to the semiarid south. Ongoing projects for utilizing new sources include cloud seeding, recycling of sewage water, and the desalination of seawater. It is said that humans can live forty days without food, three days without water, and eight minutes without air, but only one second without hope—which is why the Western Wall is so important.

"As a Jew, I need Israel. More precisely: I can live as a Jew outside Israel, but not without Israel." *~Elie Wiesel*

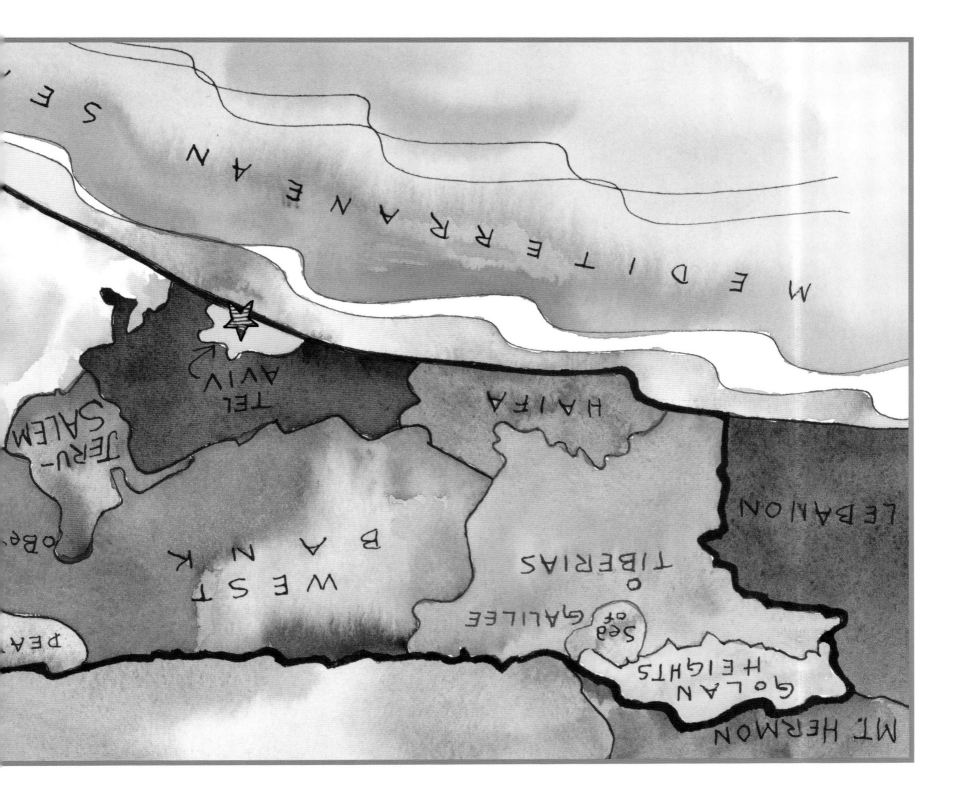

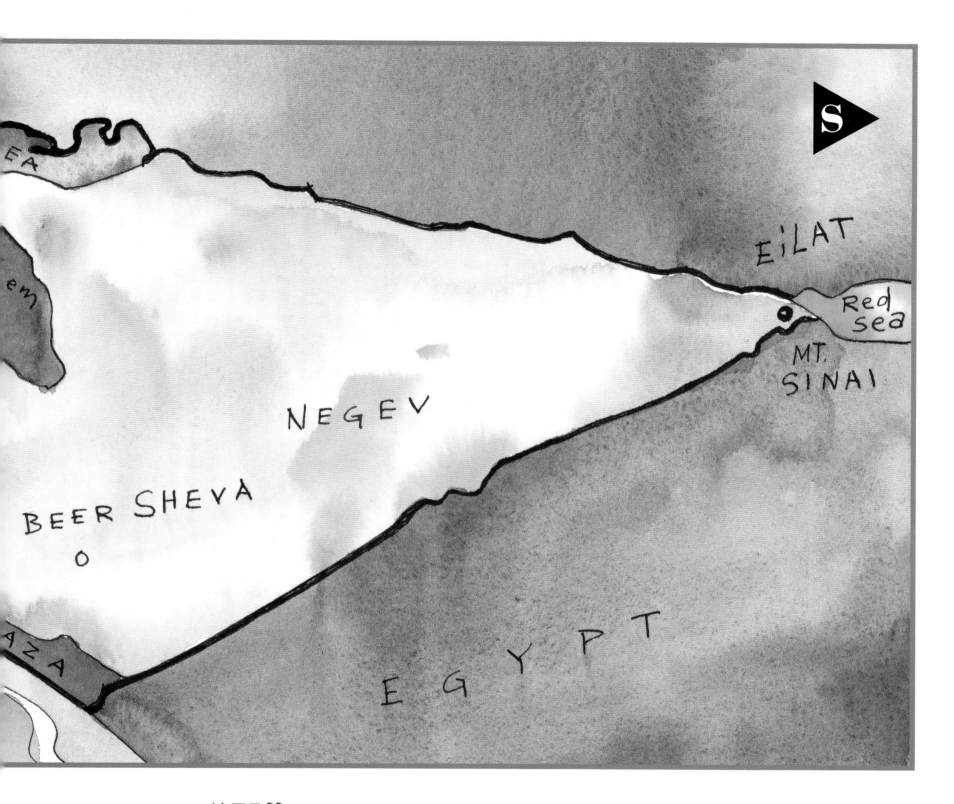

"X" marks the spot of these cool and amazing sites.

From way down south in Eilat, to the tip-top of the Golan Heights.

"Y" stands for

Yad Vashem,

A museum like no other,

A place that we are obliged to remember

A cousin, father, sibling, or mother.

From 1939 to 1945, 12 million human beings, including 6 million Jews and 1.5 million children, died in the Holocaust. Situated on Jerusalem's Mount of Remembrance, Yad Vashem's 45-acre campus comprises indoor museums, outdoor monuments, memorials, gardens, sculptures, and a world-class research and education center. These are all necessary components for a meaningful and dynamic commemoration of the Holocaust, including its victims and heroes, artifacts, survivors' testimonies, and archival material. Our task is to continuously weave personal stories into the historical narrative…and we are obliged to remember because one day soon there will be no survivors left to tell their stories.

"My heart is in the East, and I am at the ends of the West." ~*Yehuda ha-Levi*

"Z" is for

Zion*ism*,

The belief in a sovereign Jewish State.

Thanks to lots and lots of hard work,

We no longer have to wait.

צ= יונות

Zionism is a Jewish political movement that, in its broadest sense, has supported the self-determination of the Jewish people in a sovereign Jewish national homeland. Since the establishment of the modern State of Israel in 1948, the Zionist movement continues primarily to advocate on behalf of the Jewish State and address threats to its continued existence and security. Unfortunately, history has demonstrated time and again the need to ensure Jewish security through such a homeland. The re-establishment of Jewish independence in Israel, after 2,000 years of struggle to overcome foreign conquest and exile, is a vindication of the fundamental concepts of the equality of nations and of self-determination. For 2,000 years we have said, "Od lo avda tikvateinu." For 2,000 years we have not lost hope…a*nd we never will.*

The neighborhood bully, he just lives to survive.

He's criticized and condemned for being alive.

He's not supposed to fight back, he's supposed to have thick skin.

He's supposed to lay down and die when his door is kicked in.

He's the neighborhood bully.

The neighborhood bully been driven out of every land.

He's wandered the earth an exiled man.

Seen his family scattered, his people hounded and torn.

He's always on trial for just being born.

He's the neighborhood bully.

~Robert Zimmerman aka Bob Dylan

So that's our Israel aleph-bet (alphabet),

Filled with pride from A to Z.

With *vision* and *wisdom*, *hope*, and *peace*,

The best is yet to be.

No part of this publication may be reproduced, stored in a retrieval system, or transmitted in any form by any means,
electronic, mechanical, photocopying, or otherwise, without the prior written permission of the publisher,
Triumph Books LLC, 542 S. Dearborn Street, Suite 750, Chicago, Illinois 60605.

This book is available in quantity at special discounts for your group or organization. For further information, contact:

Triumph Books LLC

542 South Dearborn Street, Suite 750

Chicago, Illinois 60605

312. 939. 3330

Fax 312. 663. 3557

ISBN 978–1–60078–677–8

Printed in China

Todah Rabbah to Ben and Noah, Susan Klingman, Mitch Rogatz, Julie Stark, the wonderful family at Am Shalom, and Triumph Books.